Libby Wants to Dump the Man Called Grump

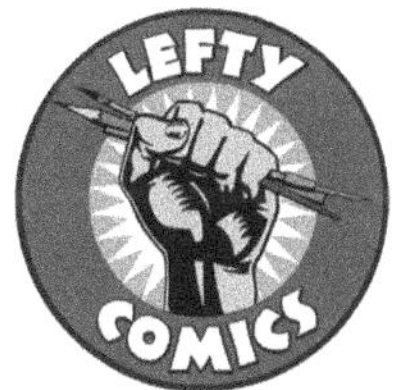

A Song by the

CULPABLY NEGLIGENT

Lefty Comics
cmebz1@yahoo.com

First Edition: July 2020

Published in North America by Lefty Comics. For information, please contact Lefty Comics at cmebz1@yahoo.com.

Library of Congress Cataloguing-In-Publication Data
Christopher Moebs
Libby Wants to Dump the Man Called Grump/Christopher Moebs– [1st] ed
p. cm.
ISBN – 978-0-578-74309-7

1. ART / Art & Politics. 2. ART / Popular Culture. 3. ART / American / General. 4. HUMOR / Form / Pictorial. 5. HUMOR / Topic / Politics. 6. MUSIC / General. 7. POLITICAL SCIENCE / Commentary & Opinion.

10 9 8 7 6 5 4 3 2 1

Comments about *Libby Wants to Dump the Man Called Grump* and requests for additional copies may be addressed to Chris Moebs via e-mail at cmebz1@yahoo.com.

Printed in the United States of America

I got a friend named Libby
She's the greatest lady I know
She hooked up with a bad hombre
He said he had a lot of dough

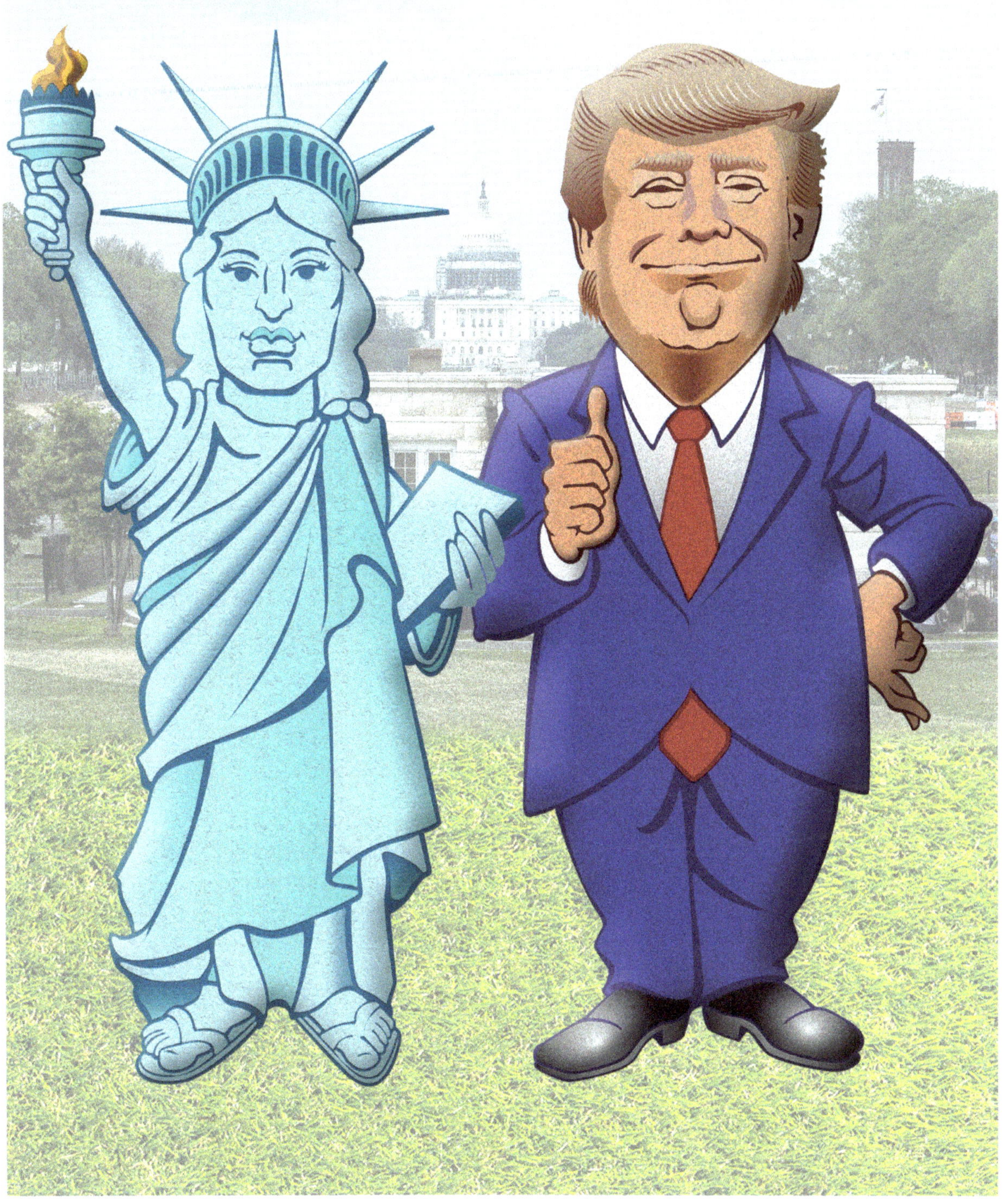

Grump insulted and abused her
He treated her like a fool
Grump called poor Libby lazy
Then spent the money she saved for school

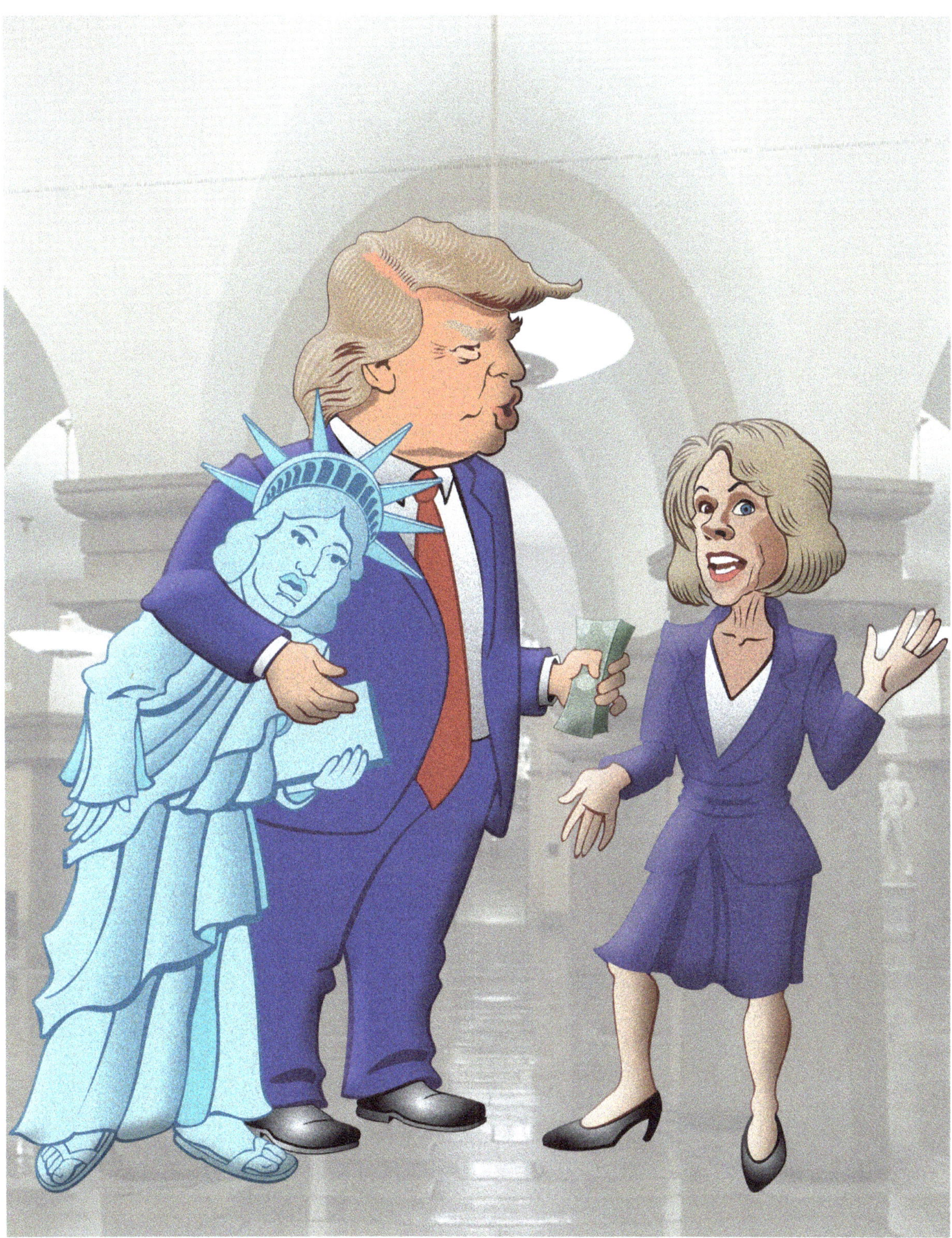

Grump broke every promise he ever made
Treated Libby's place like a dump
That's when I told her good gosh almighty girl
You need to Dump That Grump!

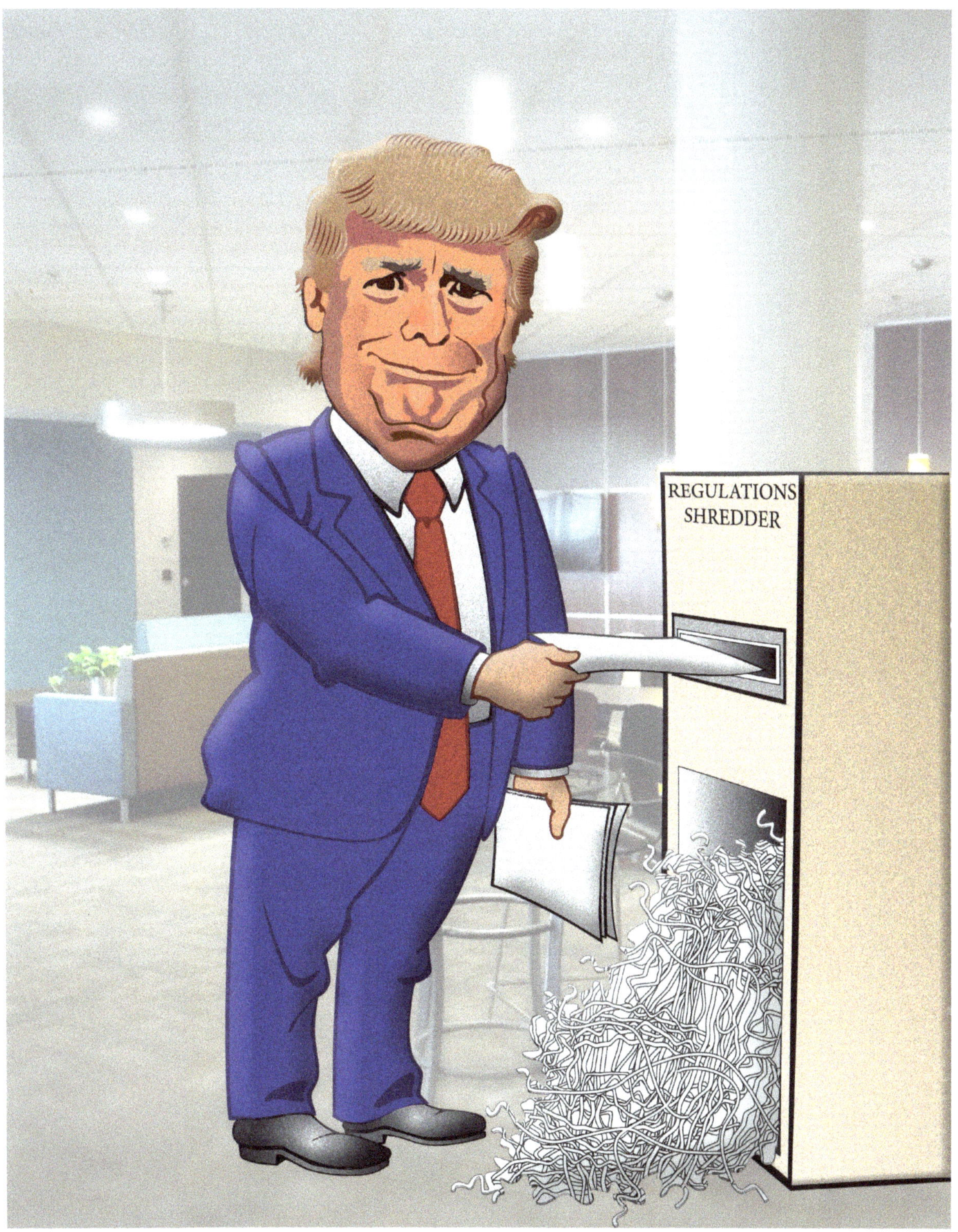
REGULATIONS
SHREDDER

Libby wants to dump the man called Grump
He's set the town on fire
Libby wants to dump the man called Grump
'Cause he's a cheater and a liar

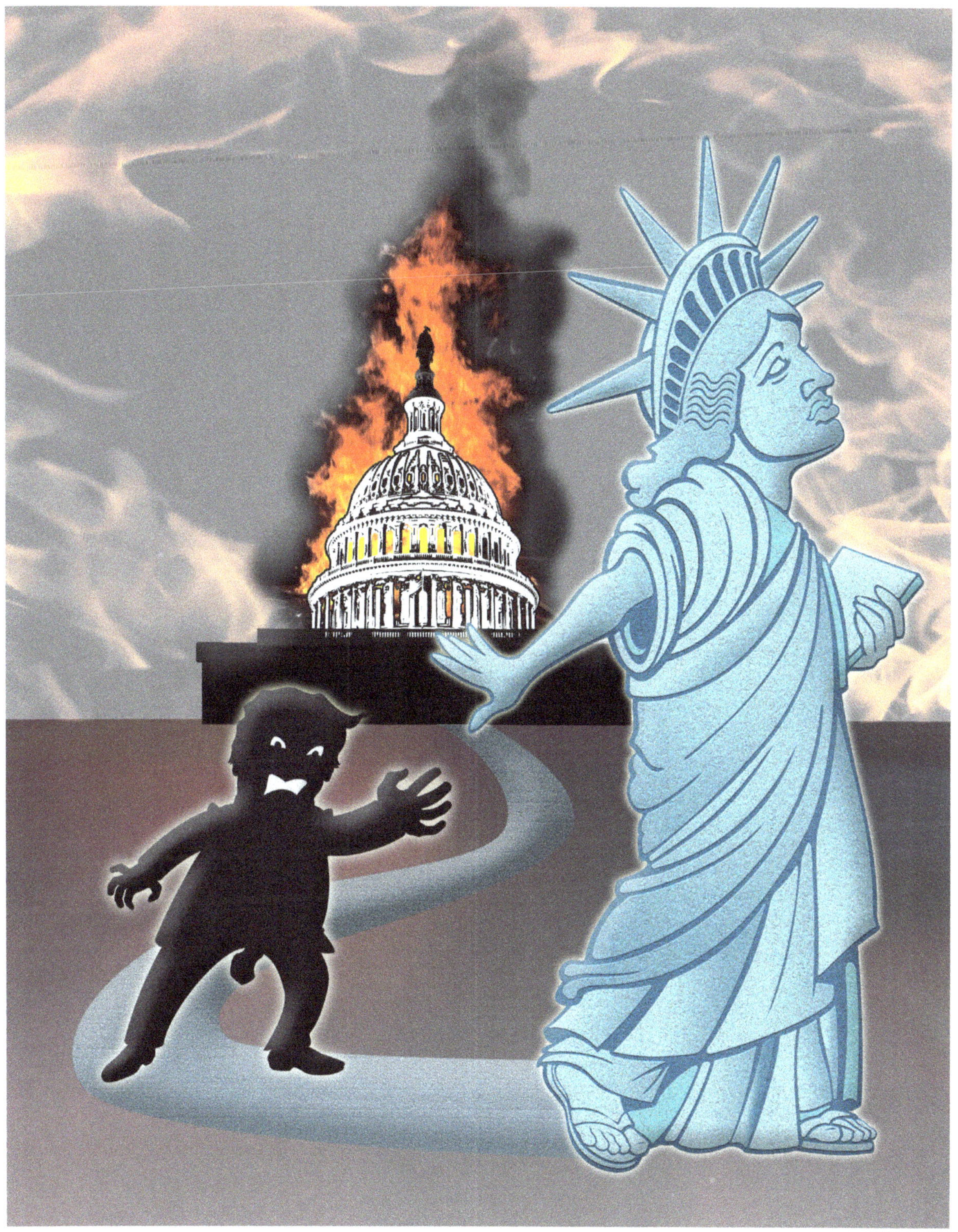

The Grump continued schemin'
His greedy plots and scams
Been a griftin' and a connin'
Since he tricked his way out of 'Nam

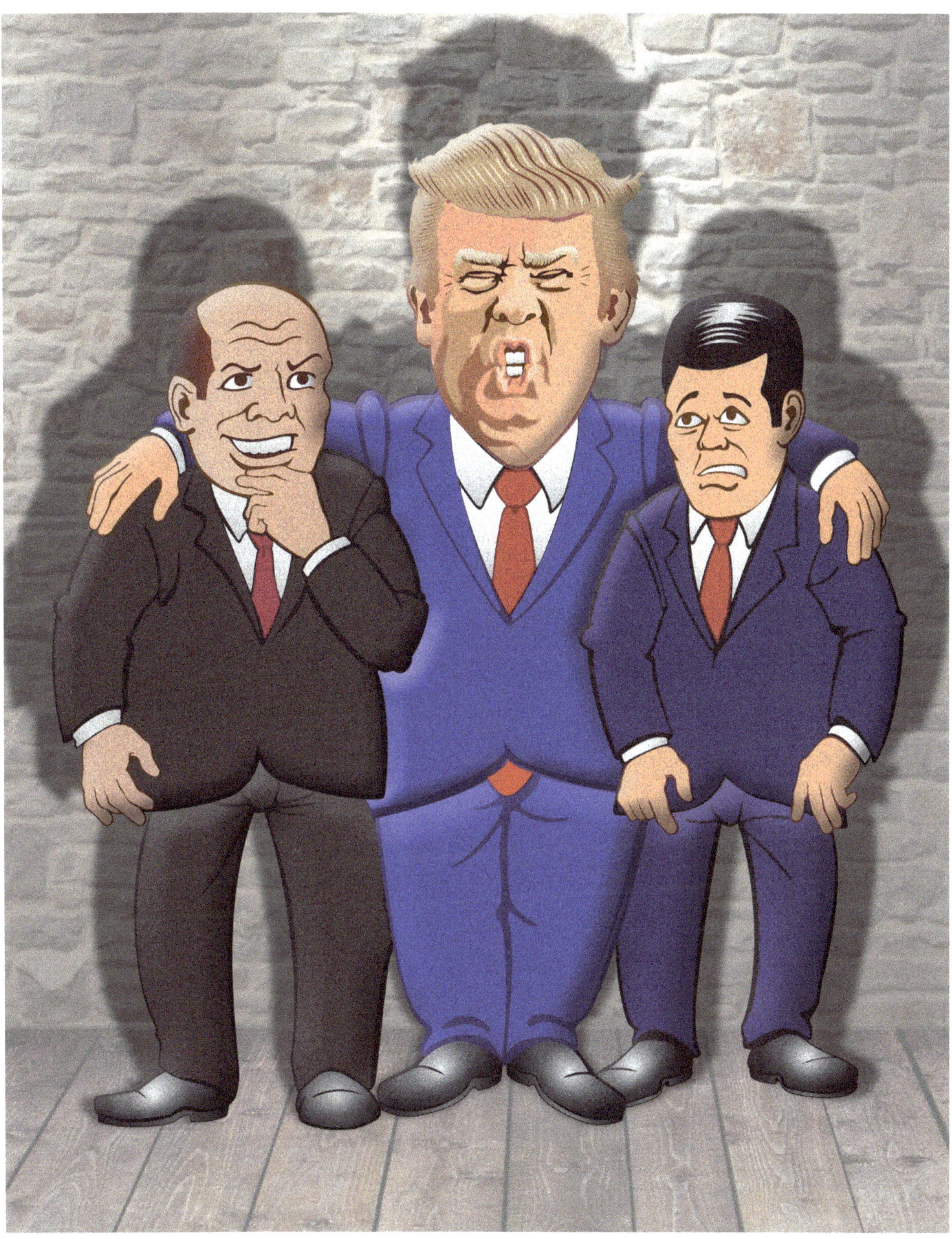

He made up tales about Libby
Accused her of all of his crimes
Grump kept on cheating and lying
Beyond all reasons and rhymes

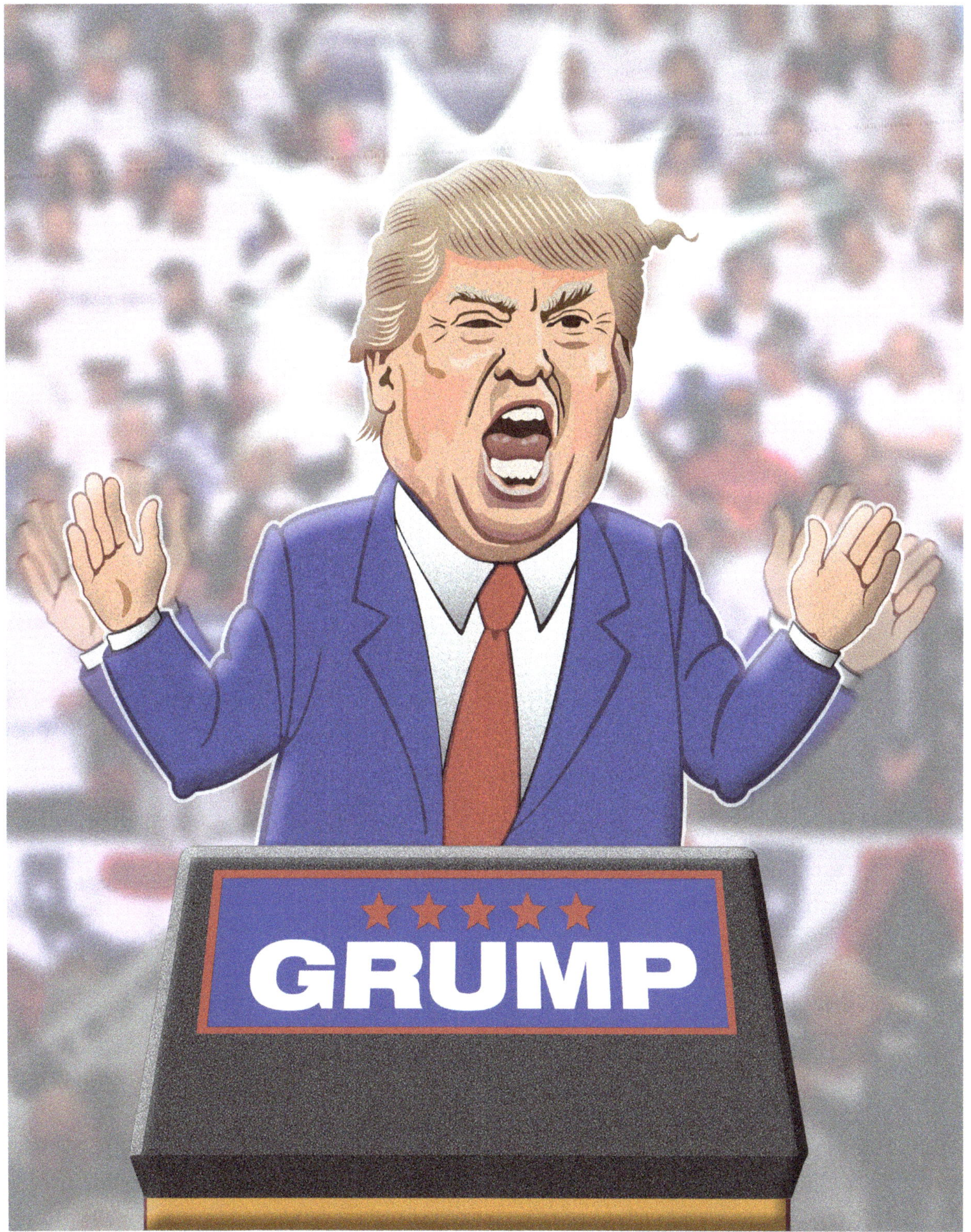
GRUMP

Inciting his pawns to violence
Scowling bully surrounded by chumps
That's when our Lady Libby said
It's time to Dump That Grump!!

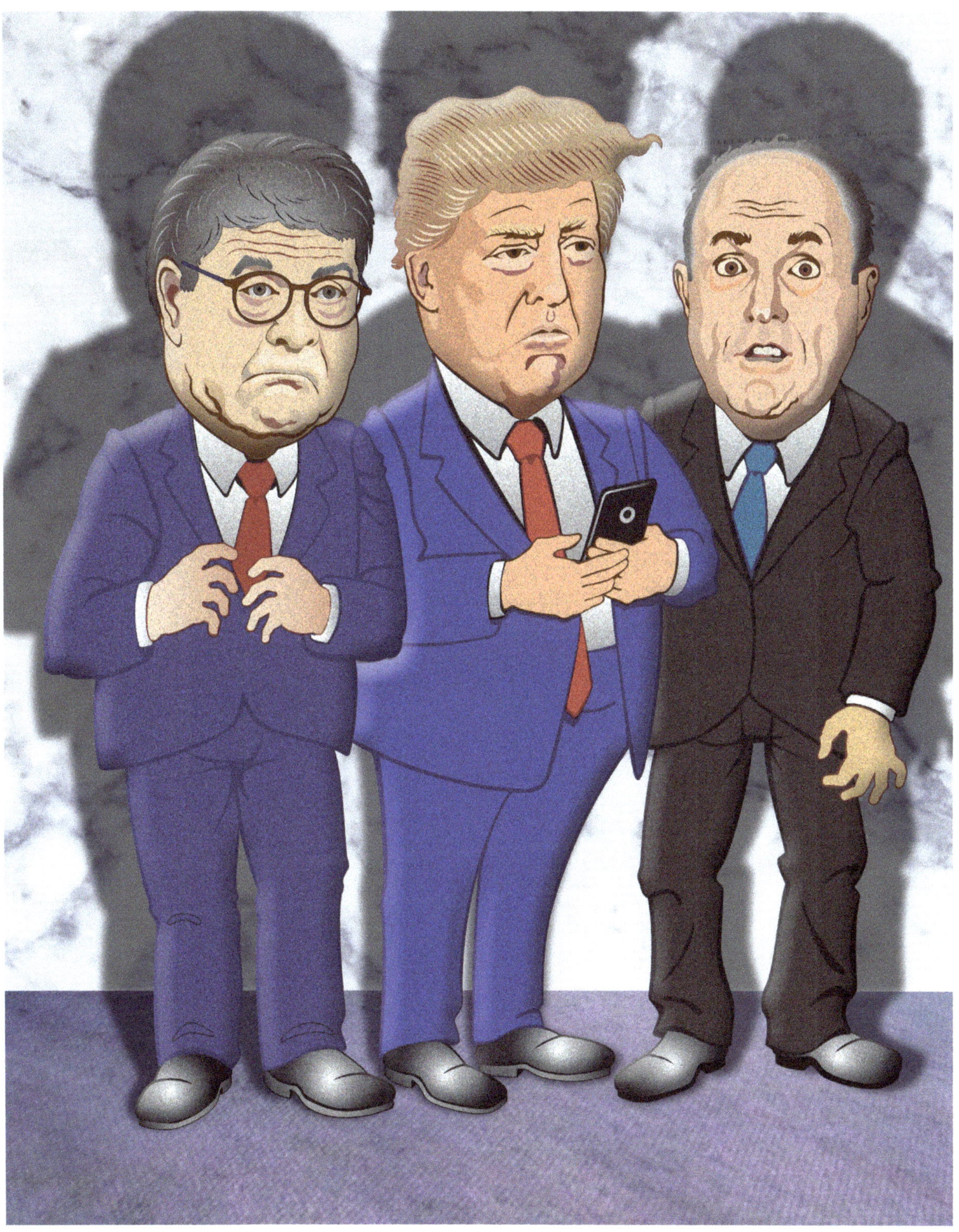

Libby wants to dump the man called Grump
He's nothing but a con
Libby wants to dump the man called Grump
And throw a party when he's gone

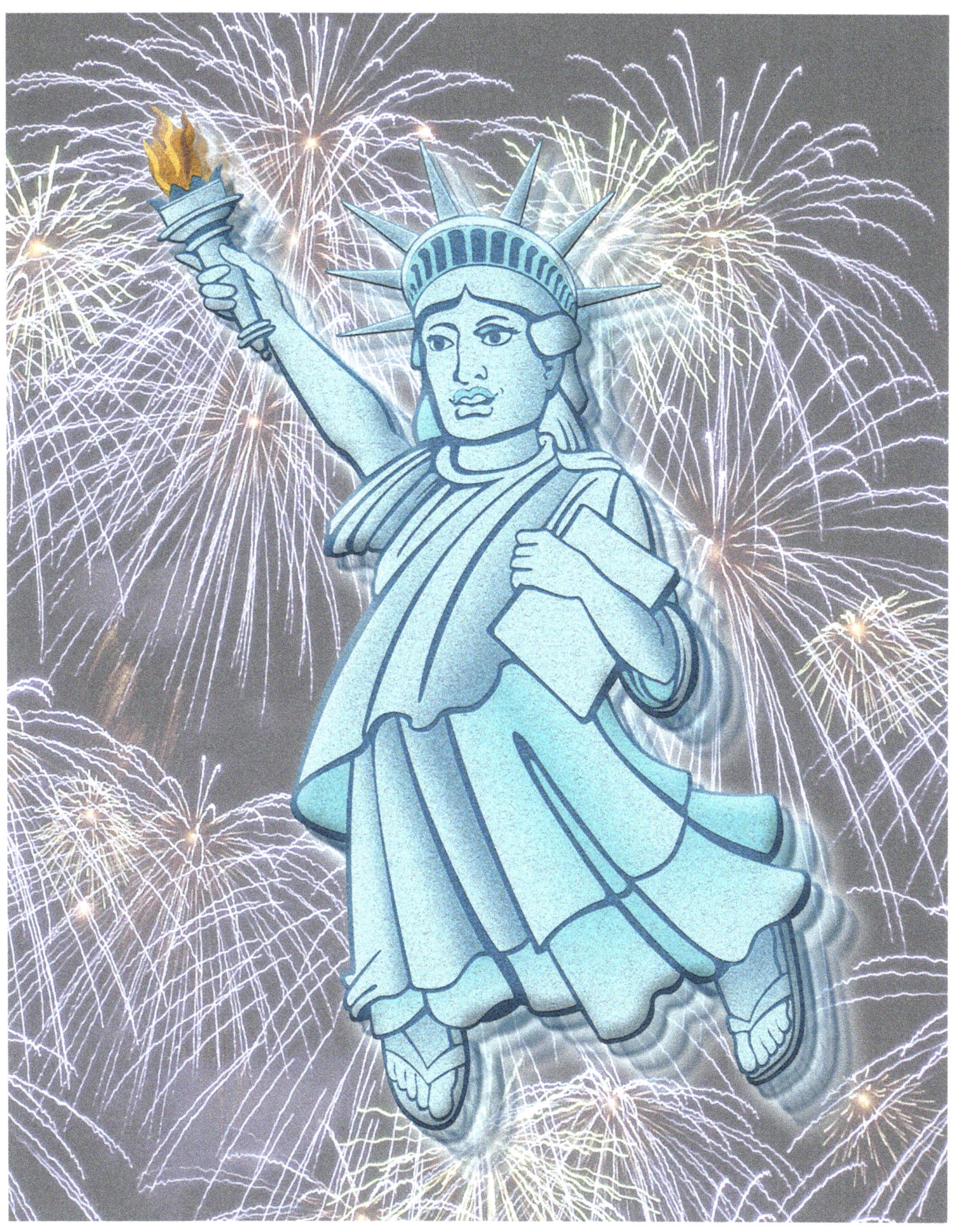

The Grump he was a divider
To cover up his conspiracies
Turned enemies into cronies
Or brought them to their knees

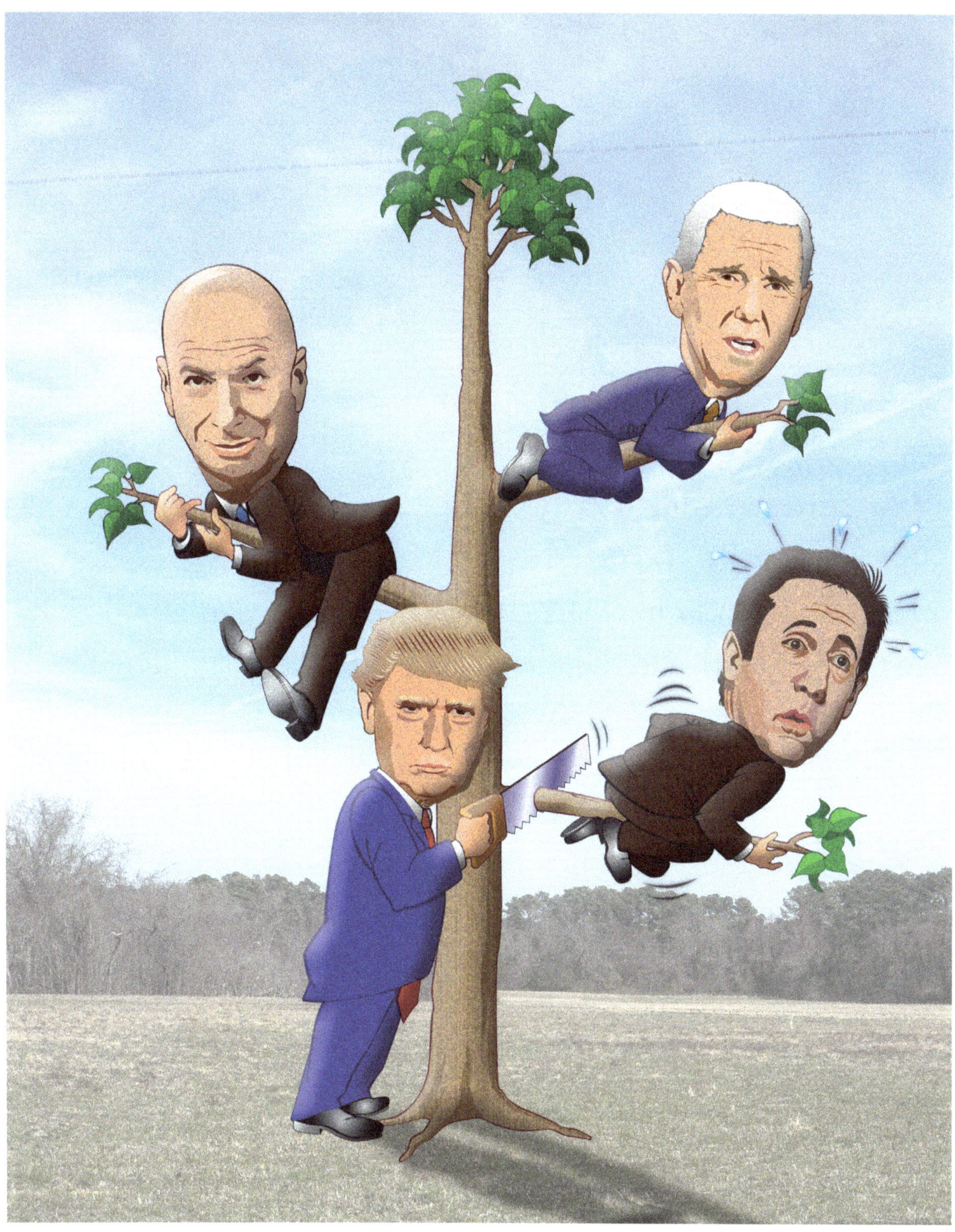

Corruption confusion and chaos
Speak loudly to hide his little stick
Building walls instead of bridges
What's good for the Grump makes Libby sick

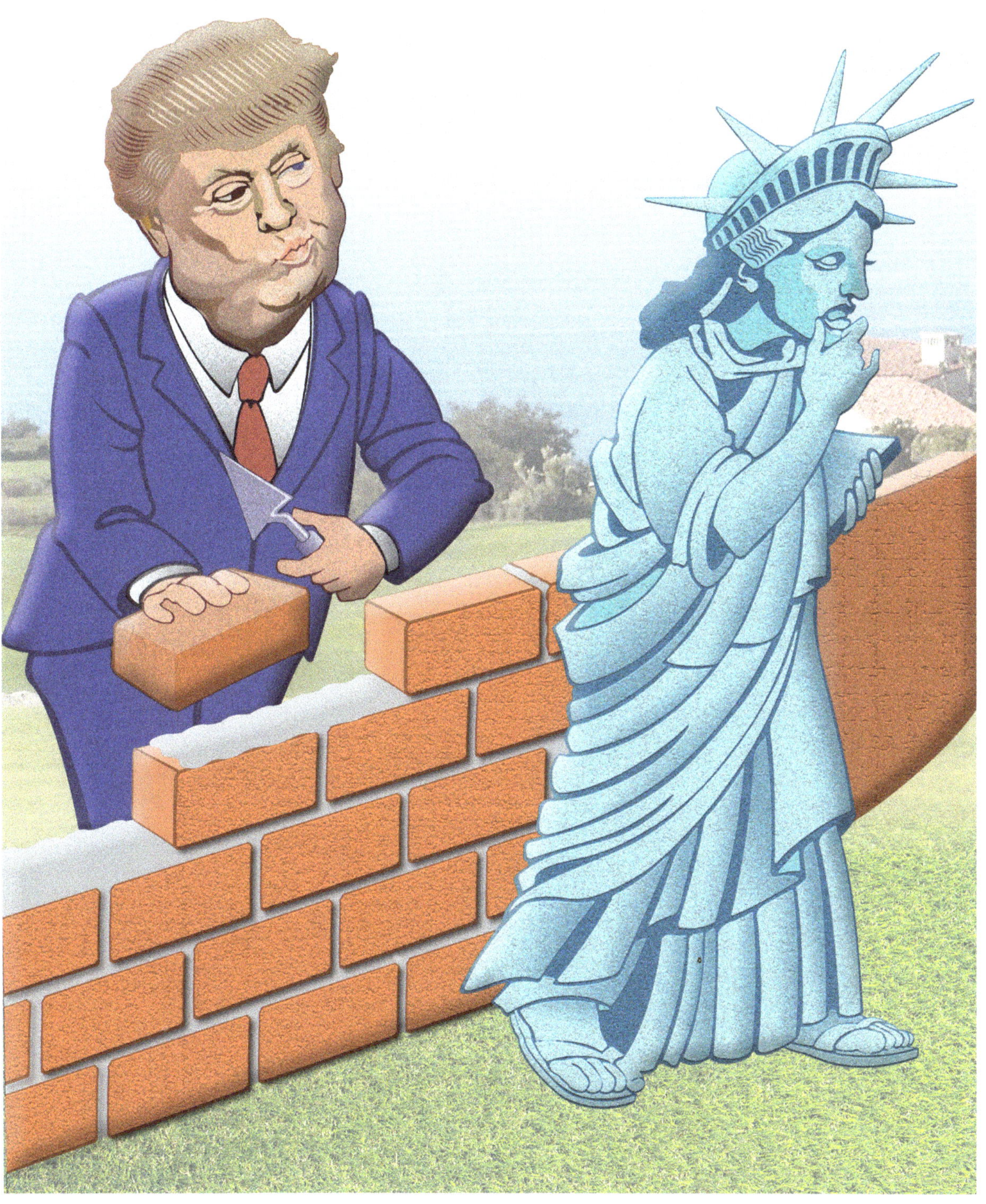

Acting tough but living in terror
Of exposure as an impotent lump
The vulgar Dotard’s time is up
She’s gonna Dump that Grump!

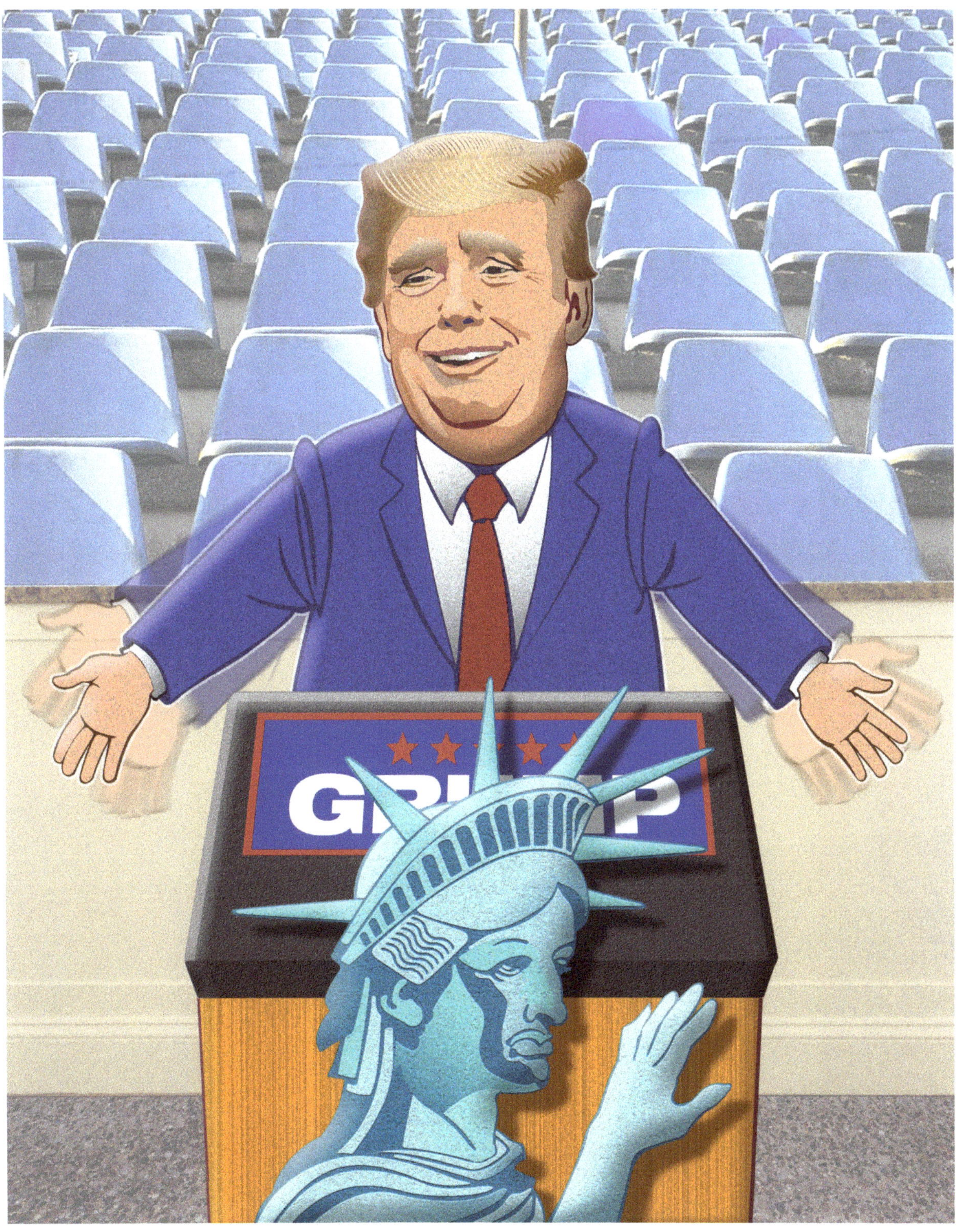

Libby wants to dump the man called Grump
He's set the town on fire
Libby wants to dump the man called Grump
'Cause he's a cheater and a liar

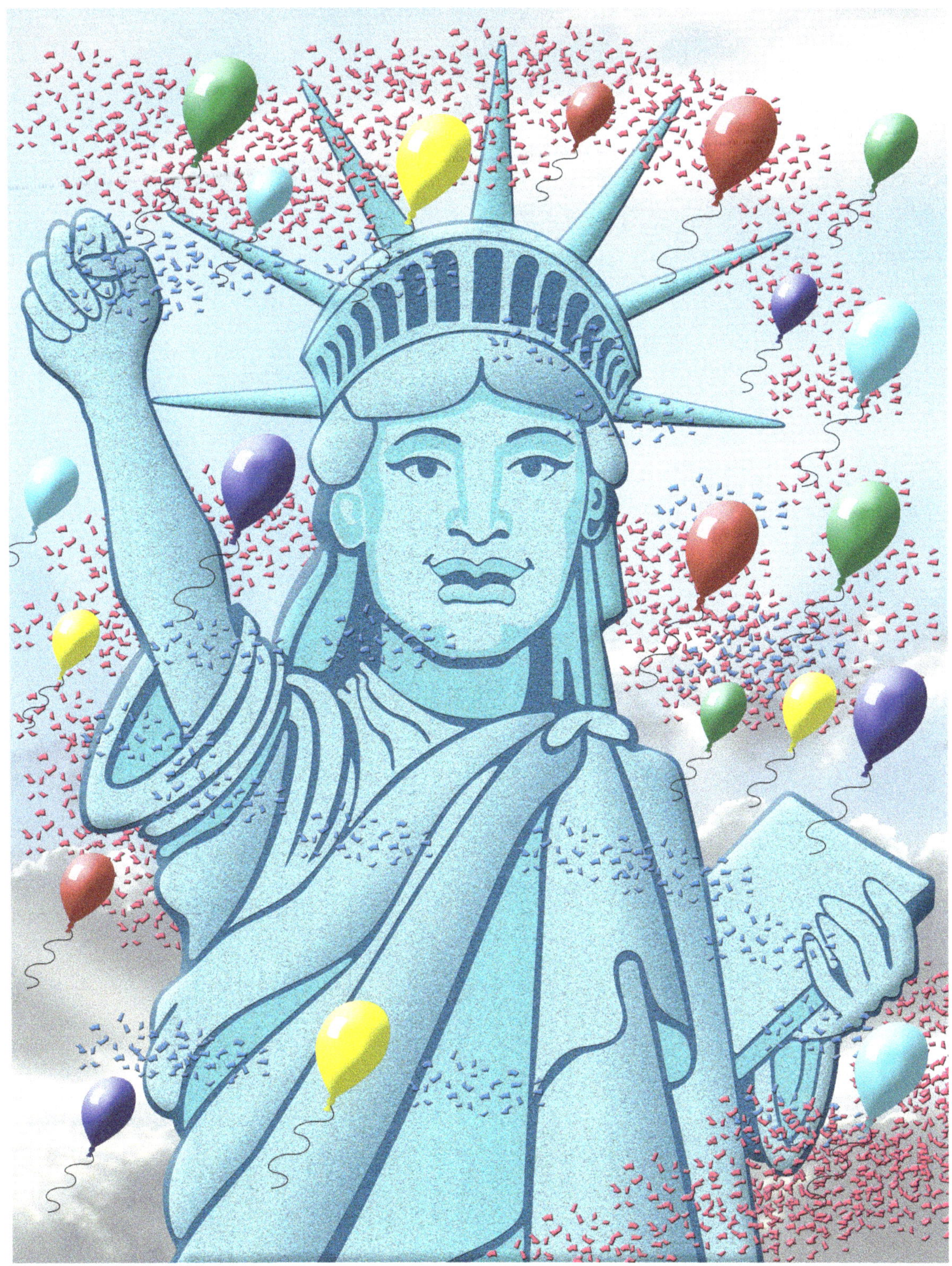

Dump that Grump!

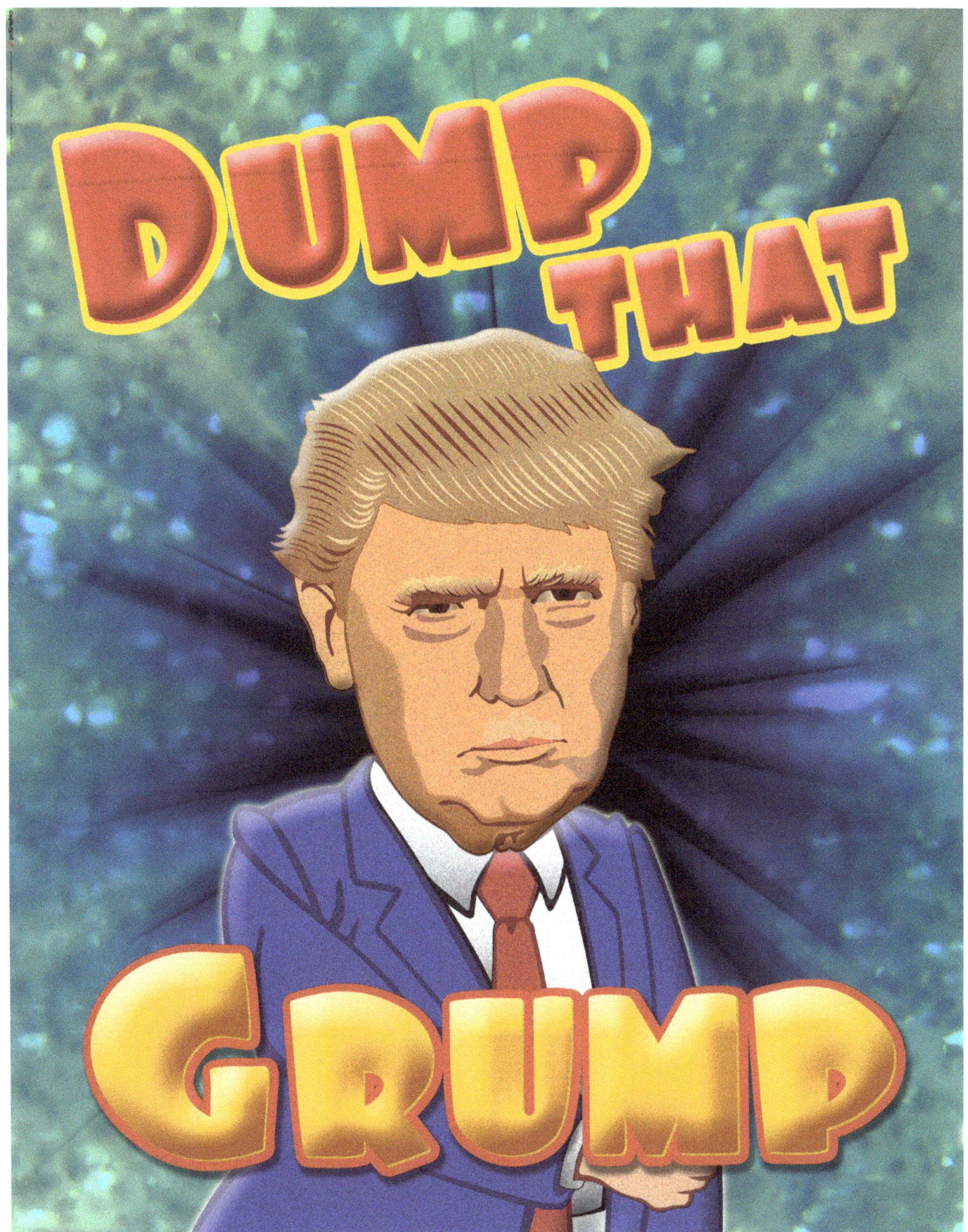
DUMP
THAT
GRUMP

www.ingramcontent.com/pod-product-compliance
Lightning Source LLC
Chambersburg PA
CBHW042054030726
47599CB00019B/2491
9780578743097